HELLO GNU, HOW DO YOU DO?

A Beginning Guide to Positively Polite Behavior

BARBARA SHOOK HAZEN

Illustrated by
DARA GOLDMAN

DOUBLEDAY
NEW YORK LONDON TORONTO SYDNEY AUCKLAND

To Brack for brave new worlds full of positive pleasures.

—The Mom

A DOUBLEDAY BOOK
Published by Delacorte Press
Bantam Doubleday Dell Publishing Group, Inc.
666 Fifth Avenue, New York, New York 10103

Doubleday and the portrayal of an anchor with a dolphin
are trademarks of Bantam Doubleday Dell Publishing Group, Inc.

Library of Congress Cataloging-in-Publication Data

Hazen, Barbara Shook.
    Hello Gnu, how do you do? : a beginning guide to positively polite
behavior / by Barbara Shook Hazen; illustrated by Dara Goldman. p.   cm.
    Summary: Animal characters in various situations show the proper
manners or behavior in such areas as visiting or giving a party,
writing thank-you notes, and showing common courtesy at home,
with friends, or at school.
    1. Etiquette for children and teenagers. [1. Etiquette.]
I. Goldman, Dara, ill. II. Title.
BJ1857.C5H3275   1990
    395'.122—dc20   89-35694   CIP   AC
ISBN 0-385-26449-6

Printed in Hong Kong
September 1990
10 9 8 7 6 5 4 3 2

DESIGNED BY—DIANE STEVENSON/SNAP-HAUS GRAPHICS

CONTENTS

GNU NOTE   5

YOUR PERSONAL BEST   6
    NICE WAYS TO BE
    LOOKING GOOD
    AT HOME
    NICE FRIENDS

SPEAKING UP   16
    CONVERSATIONAL COURTESIES
    MAGIC WORDS
    GREETINGS
    INTRODUCTIONS
    ON THE TELEPHONE
    ANSWERING THE DOORBELL

IN PUBLIC   26
    IN A THEATER
    IN A STORE
    IN THE PARK
    AT THE LIBRARY, AT A MUSEUM, OR IN CHURCH
    AT THE HOSPITAL
    AT A WEDDING
    AT A FUNERAL

SCHOOL DAYS, POLITE WAYS   36

GOOD MANNERS MAKE GOOD SPORTS   38

MOVABLE MANNERS — 40
IN A CAR
ON AN AIRPLANE
ON A BUS

PARTY TIME — 42
PLANNING AND INVITING
GIVING A PARTY

GIFT GIVING AND GETTING — 46

LETTER PERFECT — 49
THANK-YOU NOTES
OTHER GNU NOTES

VISITING — 52
WHEN YOU VISIT
WHEN A FRIEND SLEEPS OVER

EAT NICELY — 54
BASIC GOOD TABLE MANNERS
TABLE TIPS
PROBLEMS, PITFALLS, AND ACCIDENTS
IN A RESTAURANT

END NOTE — 62

GNU NOTE

Dear Friend,

Good manners, like good-night hugs and good-morning smiles, are happy habits.

Caring—for each other, for property, and for our world—is their common root. Caring makes you want to eat nicely, so that others will want to sit next to you. Caring makes you want to share, lend a helping hand or paw, and put your banana peels in the trash can.

Good manners soothe hurts, nourish friendships, and smooth everyday life. They please others while making you more well-liked.

Consideration is the key word. The basic rule of polite behavior is to treat others as you would like to be treated. You can't go wrong if you do that.

Still, it is nice to know the specifics of what to do, whether eating, introducing, or sending party invitations. There are tricks, tips, and proper ways to do things. Knowing them makes whatever you do more fun, and makes you more secure.

My Gnu Rules are based on doing, not don't-ing. Their purpose is to increase pleasure and show you how to be positively polite.

Enjoy!

Your Gnu friend,
Nicky

YOUR PERSONAL BEST

NICE WAYS TO BE

Nicky Gnu tries to behave certain ways every day.

He is *thoughtful.* He thinks about the feelings and wishes of others. He reads instead of playing the drums when his father has a headache and his mother is paying bills.

He is *neat.* He picks up his skates, his blocks, his People Village, and his sweater so the living room looks nice, and nobody, including himself, slips and trips.

He is *generous*. He shares his birthday bonbons with Sis Gnu even though he could eat them all.

In return, she lets him use her sled.

Nicky is *prompt*. When asked to come or do something *now*, he does.

Coming, Mom Gnu.

He is *careful* with what belongs to others. He brings Sis Gnu's borrowed crayon back in good condition, and he puts it back in its proper place.

He is *cheerful* and *pleasant*, even when it's raining too hard to play outside, and his block tower falls, and Oopsa Elephant can't come over to play, and he is coming down with the sniffles.

P. S. GNU NOTE:
He doesn't always succeed but he *always* tries.

LOOKING GOOD

Looking good makes Nicky Gnu feel good.

That's why he combs his hair, brushes his teeth, puts on clean clothes, and cleans his paws—under the nails too—before he goes anyplace, even downstairs to breakfast.

He holds his head high, walks tall, and smiles a lot. A face is a window that reflects what's inside. Nicky's smile reflects his pleasure in being well-groomed.

Iggy Ape gets up too late to take a bath, tosses on yesterday's clothes over his pajamas, doesn't even try to comb his hair, and slouches downstairs feeling grouchy and grrrrrowly.

Who wants to sit next to him? Nobody.

AT HOME

Home manners may be more casual than manners used in public, but courtesy is even more important in close quarters. Nicky Gnu sometimes kicks up his heels, but he is never rude or rowdy, and he is careful not to go near Mom Gnu's precious breakable ornaments.

Nicky doesn't make extra work. He wipes his muddy hooves before he comes inside and hangs up his jacket so Mom Gnu won't have to pick up after him.

He is respectful and considerate. He doesn't stand *every* time Gram Gnu trots into the room. But he does get up and offer her the cozy chair so she can sit more comfortably.

Where family property, like the TV, is concerned, Nicky and Sis Gnu take turns watching their favorite shows.

When Dad Gnu wants to watch the Gnu News, Nicky cheerfully accepts "grown-ups first." He'll be one too someday.

Nicky thanks Sis Gnu for feeding Goldy Fish when he gallops out to play and forgets.

When she has someone over, he puts away his drums and plays quietly. He doesn't peek at her Top Secret diary even though he's tempted. He knows that respecting someone's privacy is important.

Nicky is a good big brother to Newie Gnu. He doesn't tease him for talking to a blanket. He leads the way and holds Newie's paw through the dark at the top of the stairs.

Nicky does his chores cheerfully, even yukky ones like scrubbing pots.

When everyone shares, the work goes quicker. Sometimes it's even fun.

NICE FRIENDS

Nicky Gnu and his friends know that the best way to have a friend is to be a friend.

Friends *cooperate*.

Lena Leopard and Zeke Zebra have totally different styles and tastes, but they go well together.

Slither may be a snake but I've never seen him do anything sneaky.

Friends are *understanding* and *stick up for each other*.

Wilma Warthog is sympathetic when Oopsa Elephant trips and tells about her bad day.

She is also *loyal*. The one thing she doesn't want to hear is anything bad about Slither Snake, who is also her friend.

Friends *appreciate each other*.

Leo Lion compliments Gloria Giraffe's skill in making baskets.

Gloria reminds Leo that he's a swift runner, and that together, they make great teammates.

Friends are *generous* and *tuned in to each other's feelings.*
Annie Anteater shares her Choco Bar with Peter Panda because the taste of friendship is even sweeter than the taste of chocolate-covered ants.

She goes up to Peter because he's too shy to ask for a bite, and because he's looks lonely.

Nicky and his friends are polite to *everyone,* even selfish Iggy, who bullies, bosses, uses bad language, and has never learned how to be a friend.

Nicky is coolly polite. He doesn't let Iggy's bad mood and manners spoil his good day.

SPEAKING UP

CONVERSATIONAL COURTESIES

Whenever Nicky Gnu opens his mouth, he tries to sound like someone nice to know.

Talking with him is happy talk because Nicky is conversationally courteous.

He *listens* attentively, *looks* at the speaker, and *waits* his turn to talk.

Conversation is like a good ball game. Everyone takes turns and no one hogs the ball.

Nicky tries not to say anything to hurt anyone's feelings. He admires Wilma Warthog's boots without commenting on her big feet.

He's good at keeping secrets and sticking up for his friends.

Iggy is a conversational disaster. He mumbles, grumbles, tells secrets, brags, and his only subject is himself.

Maybe that's why he's talking, unhappily, to himself.

MAGIC WORDS

Magic words have magic results. They make daily life smoother and everyone happier.

Nicky Gnu and his friends make using them a happy habit.

PLEASE, MAY I are the magic words used to ask for something or request permission.

CAN I asks, am I physically able?

THANK YOU are the magic words to show appreciation for a present, a special outing, a helping hand, or a favor, like your sister letting you use her bike.

YOU'RE WELCOME shows appreciation for being thanked.

I'M SORRY is what to say when you've spilled or spoiled something, behaved badly, are late, or want to show sympathy.

EXCUSE ME and PARDON ME are the magic words to say when unavoidably inconveniencing others, as when cutting into a conversation, cutting dinner short, or cutting in front of someone.

GREETINGS

A greeting is the polite way to begin and end the day, and to recognize friends and family.

Smile, say the name, and look the someone you're greeting in the eye.

INTRODUCTIONS

Introducing is the warm way to share friends and bring new friends together.

Nicky Gnu has a trick for remembering whose name to say first. It is *Important older women first.*

He says the name of the more important someone first.

He says the name of the older before the younger if both are equally important.

He says the woman's name first if everything else is equal.

He also introduces himself at school and at parties.

Admiral Bird, I'd like you to meet my mother.

Gram Gnu, this is Miss Gazelle. She's my gym teacher at school.

Hi, I'm Nicky Gnu from Gnutown. Where are you from? And what is your favorite sport? Gnutown has a great playground. May I show you around?

GNU NOTES

Stand when introducing or being introduced.

Shake any paw or hand offered. (It's polite to offer yours to a grown-up.)

Use titles such as Doctor, Professor, President, Aunt, or Admiral.

It's nice to tell the somebodies you're introducing something about each other.

Say something gracious after being introduced, such as "It's nice to meet you," or "I've always wanted to meet a platypus from Podunk who plays trombone. Maybe we can play together."

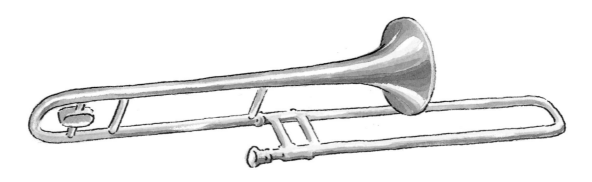

ON THE TELEPHONE

When the telephone rings, Nicky Gnu answers it politely. He says "Hello" in a clear voice that sounds as if he is smiling, which he is.

The call is for Mom Gnu, so he says, "Just a minute, please. I'll tell her."

Mom Gnu is up to her paws in paint and can't talk now.
So Nicky asks if he can take a message.
He takes the caller's name and number and the message. He repeats everything to make sure he wrote it down correctly, and sees that Mom Gnu gets the message promptly.

When Nicky calls Pamela Peacock, he dials carefully. He says, "Hello, Mrs. Peacock, this is Nicky Gnu," when Pamela's mother answers. (He would say, "Hi, Pam, this is Nicky Gnu," if he recognized his friend's voice.)

When Pamela comes to the phone, Nicky gets to the point of his call quickly, because it isn't thoughtful to tie up the line. (If Pamela were out, Nicky would leave his name and a brief message, such as, "Could Pam please call me tonight about the math homework?")

Iggy Ape always calls during mealtimes, gets bubble gum on the telephone, and mumbles, "Guess who?"

Mostly, his friends can, because Iggy sounds as ill-mannered as he looks and acts.

ANSWERING THE DOORBELL

When the front doorbell rings, Nicky Gnu is *courteous* and *cautious.*

He doesn't answer it unless Mom or Dad Gnu says it's okay.

He doesn't ask anyone in who isn't a friend, neighbor, or relative.

Nicky greets his mother's best friend with a friendly, "Hello, Mrs. Anteater. Won't you please come in. Make yourself comfortable while I tell Mom Gnu you're here."

Nicky does not ask the Zip-Quick delivery zebra in. He asks, "What is it, please?" through the locked screen door.

When told there is a jumbo jar of jelly beans for his father, Nicky tells the delivery zebra to "Please wait. I'll tell Dad Gnu you're here."

IN PUBLIC

Public places are for everybody. In them Nicky Gnu and his friends are extra polite because misbehavior stands out like a sore paw.

He suits his behavior to the situation. He yells "Go, Green Team!" at the big school game. But he doesn't make a sound at Gloria's song recital, except to clap afterward.

IN A THEATER

Annie Anteater sits quietly, paws folded on her lap. She watches the show attentively and doesn't crunch candied ants during the quiet parts.

She makes it easy for Oopsa Elephant to get by, and saves comments about the show for later.

Iggy Ape tries unsuccessfully to *be* the show. He kicks the seat in front, takes an extra seat for his jacket, rattles candy wrappers, spills his soda on his neighbor, and yells so loudly an usher is about to usher him out.

IN A STORE

At the Gnu Supermarket, Nicky steers the cart carefully and touches only what he intends to buy. He asks Mom Gnu for what he wants without whining or begging, and accepts her "No" without a fuss.

Gogo Tiger feels like pushing ahead in the checkout line but doesn't. He lets Ozzie Otter, who has one item, go ahead and he makes a new friend.

Oopsa carries Mother Elephant's grocery bag, and holds the door for her.

Leo Lion amuses himself without tugging at Mama Lion's tail or acting growly when she stops to chat with an old friend.

Iggy Ape races his cart, screams, "Bananas now!" and starts a fruit avalanche when he crash-lands.

The store manager tells him he'll have to pay for what he's spoiled, and never to come back please, *ever*.

IN THE PARK

Wild Wood Park is a very special place. Nicky Gnu and his friends care about keeping it that way.

Nicky Gnu wipes the crayoned initials I.A. off General Gnu's snout. Statues are public property and public property should never be defaced. It is there for *everyone* to enjoy.

Vandalism isn't funny, which is why Iggy isn't allowed inside.

General Gnu
Founder of Wildwood

Annie Anteater stashes her plastic candied-ant wrappers in the trash basket.

Littering is rude and inconsiderate, and plastic wrappers look awful forever. Annie does her part to keep the park nice and natural.

Oopsa Elephant admires but doesn't paw or pick the rare flute-flowered fern.

She doesn't do anything to scare off the even rarer Leaping Lizard either.

Wasn't she lucky to see both! Her being quiet helped.

Gogo Tiger keeps to the right on the bike path and watches out for others, especially smaller others.

Leo Lion cleans his brush with a napkin, not in Fish Pond. He knows paint and foreign objects pollute, and could kill the fish.

AT THE LIBRARY, AT A MUSEUM, OR IN CHURCH

In the library, Nicky Gnu whispers when he has to ask a question. He treats the books like friends, and brings back any he borrows on time in case someone else is waiting to read them.

In a museum, Nicky keeps his voice down, his footsteps careful. He doesn't lean on the glass cases or paw any of the precious things.

He doesn't try to push in front. He waits his turn to see the rare dinosaur egg, then steps thoughtfully aside to let others look.

32

In a place of worship, Nicky is respectful and attentive. He watches his parents when he's not sure whether to stand or sit.

He doesn't wriggle, whisper to Sis Gnu, kick the seat in front, or play with the robot in his pocket even when his thoughts wander.

AT THE HOSPITAL

Oopsa Elephant has a terrible case of poison ivory. When Nicky Gnu visits Oopsa in the hospital, he arrives at the proper visiting hour, keeps his voice down, is pleasant to the Aardvark sharing her room, and obeys hospital procedure.

He does everything he can to make Oopsa feel better.

He cranks up her bed and brings her a straw.

He tells Oopsa a Purple People joke, which makes her laugh.

He brings Oopsa a book for now and a Swamp-O bar for later when she feels better.

He fills her in on what's going on and tells her how much she is missed.

Knowing she's missed and has such a caring friend makes Oopsa feel better.

AT A WEDDING

At ceremonies and formal occasions, Nicky Gnu lets his feelings show and his behavior reflect the occasion.

Nicky's teacher, Miss Armadillo, is getting married and he is invited to the wedding.

He puts on his best suit and his best behavior. He watches the grown-ups, and sits and stands when they do.

He successfully stifles a giggle when Miss Armadillo's father almost trips on her veil. He doesn't want to laugh out loud or do anything to spoil the bride's day.

At the wedding reception, Nicky shakes the groom's paw, kisses the bride, and says something nice like, "You make a great couple!"

Later he drinks party punch, eats wedding cake without dropping a crumb, and waltzes with the bride.

AT A FUNERAL

When Great-Grand-Gnu dies, Nicky goes to the funeral, the memorial service in her honor.

During the service he is quiet and respectful. He remembers Great-Grand-Gnu's stories about when she was little, her dandelion bread, the fun he had visiting her, their games of Hide and Peek, and lots of other things that were special about her.

He feels sad, and glad too—glad that she was his Great-Grand-Gnu and that he knew her. He will always remember her.

SCHOOL DAYS, POLITE WAYS

School is the place to learn new things, make new friends, and practice good manners.

Nicky Gnu tries to be on time to school, with his books and finished homework. He greets his teacher with a friendly "Good morning, Mrs. Armadillo." He knows teachers have feelings too.

Oopsa listens, *really* listens, in class. She is quick to help when something needs to be done.

I was new once too.

Peter Panda is shy. It's hard for him to speak up in class, though he does. He knows how the new kid feels. That's why he makes a special effort to talk to him and show him around.

Leo Lion keeps his voice down when he walks through the halls even though he feels like roaring and running. He'll do that during recess.

See. Look at me.

Prissa Panther brings golden apples to impress the teacher. She brags a lot about her perfect grades and perfect manners.

No one is impressed, because no one is perfect. Prissa would be better liked if she were naturally polite.

Iggy Ape laughs at everyone else's mistakes, disrupts the classroom, snitches pencils, and cheats.

The one he cheats most is himself, because he doesn't learn, make friends, or like school.

GOOD MANNERS MAKE GOOD SPORTS

Nicky Gnu is a good sport. Fun and friendship are more important to him than winning, though he likes to win too.

When Gogo Tiger wins the high jump, he shakes Gogo's paw and congratulates him. Gogo resists bragging, "Wow, wasn't I wonderful." Instead he says, "Good try and good fun."

Oopsa Elephant is a good sport too. She joins the others skating even though she prefers indoor sports and is a total klutz.

She can't skate but she tries. And she is fun to be with because she can laugh at herself.

After her tenth trip, Leo Lion gives her a lesson and his paw. Good sports look out for each other.

38

Iggy is a terrible sport. He is a sore loser and boastful winner. (He won the skate race by starting before the gun and tripping Zeke Zebra.)

Now he's whining, "I'm cold, and I want to go home unless we play my way."

"GO!" everyone agrees. Poor sports and cheaters aren't missed. They just spoil the fun for others.

MOVABLE MANNERS

Going places with Nicky Gnu is a pleasure because he is a good traveler, who likes new places and new experiences.

Above all, Nicky is a good sport, even when Jungle World is closed and plans have to be changed.

Because he is such a good traveler, he gets taken lots of places.

IN A CAR

On an outing in the new blue Gnumobile, Nicky keeps his voice down and saves kicking up his hooves for later. In a car, moving around can be dangerous, and safety and courtesy go together.

Nicky keeps his window up because Gram Gnu is cold. He keeps his seat belt fastened at all times.

He enjoys himself quietly, watching the passing scene, playing word games with Sis Gnu, and helping Dad Gnu watch for Gnu Pond signs.

He doesn't bicker or whine, "I'm hungry. I want a McBiggie," even though he is hungry. Guess what? As a treat Dad Gnu stops at McBiggie's, because he's made extra-good time due to everybody's extra-good behavior.

ON AN AIRPLANE

There isn't much room on a plane. Even the food dishes are small.

Nicky tucks his paws in, and whispers so as not to disturb his neighbor, who is taking a catnap.

ON A BUS

Nicky has his fare ready before he gets on, so he won't hold up the line.

He stands back to let Gram Gnu go first.

He waves, but doesn't shout, "Yoo-hoo!" when he sees someone he knows on the bus.

He sits with his hooves tucked in, his school bag on his lap. He doesn't say anything when a hippopotamus accidentally steps on his toes.

PARTY TIME

PLANNING AND INVITING

Nicky is a real party animal. He loves to entertain. His recipe for a successful party is based on good fun, good food, and good friends.

Before giving a party for Oopsa, Nicky gets his parents' permission and plans carefully—what kind of party, what kind of food and games, and how many guests.

He sends out the party invitations several weeks ahead.

All invitations include the party giver's name, the date and time, the place, and any special information about what kind of party, and what to wear or bring.

Nicky Gnu invites *you*
to *his* surprise birthday party for
Oopsa Elephant
on **Saturday,**
October 31st, at 5 p.m.
at 20 Lilac Lane, Gnutown.
**Wear a costume since her birthday's on Hallowe'en and shhhhh,
don't tell Oopsa.
R.S.V.P. 123-4567**

Nicky helps prepare for the party by blowing up balloons, picking up his toys, decorating the table, and taste-testing the cake icing.

G N U   N O T E:

Nicky's guests R.S.V.P. (Respond Soon Very Politely) Those who can come call or write, repeating the time, the date, and the address.

Hank Hyena, who can't come, regrets politely while thanking Nicky for the invitation. He thoughtfully sends Oopsa a homemade card so she feels remembered.

GIVING A PARTY

Nicky Gnu is a good host. He does everything he can to make his guests comfortable and happy.

He greets each guest at the door. He points out the bathroom and where to put any coats and presents.

He introduces guests who don't know each other.

He spends some time with all of his guests and sees that everyone has a party hat and a good time.

He serves his guests first, and the guest of honor first of all.

He sets the tone of the party, which is lively but never out of control, which is why he's telling Iggy, "Please stop screaming and swinging on the chandelier."

When the party's over, Nicky sees each guest to the door and says, "Thank you for coming."

After the last guest goes, he gives Mom Gnu a thank-you hug and helps her tidy up.

GIFT GIVING AND GETTING

While Oopsa received many nice gifts for her birthday, there are other times besides birthdays when gift giving is appropriate, such as on holidays and when visiting.

But a gift doesn't need a reason. A just-because-I-felt-like-it or Happy Gnu Year gift has the extra pleasure of being unexpected.

A gift from the heart makes both giver and receiver happy.

Chocolate-covered ants are not to Nicky's taste, but he knows Annie loves them, so that's what he brings her on her birthday.

Annie appreciates Nicky's thoughtfulness and says, "Thank you, Nicky. They look delicious."

She doesn't say, "I already have two boxes and would have preferred grasshoppers," because that would hurt Nicky's feelings. It is the loving thought behind the gift that counts.

Oopsa Elephant doesn't have any money to buy a Mother's Day gift for her mother, so she crayons a card that says, "Good for a week's dishwashing," which pleases Mother Elephant immensely.

When Uncle Lion asks Leo what he wants for Christmas, Leo greedily says, "Earth City with all the windup cars and toy people and everything."

Earth City is very expensive, so Leo gets socks, which are useful but not much fun. Next time he'll mention several less expensive toys or books, so that Uncle Lion can choose among them.

Gogo Tiger loves to make things. He makes paper flowers and gives them to his friends with hand-decorated gift poems.

Homemade gifts and personal touches are always nice.

I think you're sweet, so here's a treat 4 U 2 eat.

Iggy gives Professor Python fancy rain boots in the hope of getting a better grade.

Professor Python thanks Iggy, who gets an F anyway.

The boots are never used, because Professor Python doesn't have feet. A gift should suit the receiver and be given without expecting something in return.

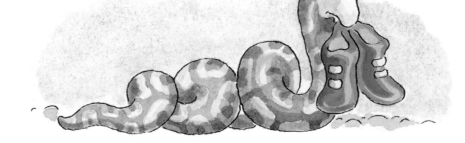

LETTER PERFECT

THANK-YOU NOTES

Nicky Gnu and his friends write an appreciative thank-you note promptly after receiving a gift or visiting someone. A thank-you note can be long or short, crayoned or written in ink. It is warm and personal. It reflects its writer's pleasure in receiving.

Sunny Sunday, November 1

Dear Nicky,

Thank you for my party. It was wonderful of you and Mom Gnu to give it for me.

I was so surprised I almost tripped on my trunk.

The food was yummy, especially the cake with your pumpkin icing.

Your gift was great. You know I love purple, and the peanut sheller is pretty and useful. I'm using it now.

What a fine friend you are!

Love and xxxxxxx,
Oopsa

P.S. Thank Mom Gnu, too, and tell Sis Gnu her elephant jokes are the greatest.

OTHER GNU NOTES

Besides writing thank-you notes, Nicky also writes to keep in touch—when he goes to camp, when a friend moves away, and when Gram Gnu goes to Sunshine Beach.

He writes neatly and naturally, and his notes are a pleasure to receive.

Dear Gram Gnu,

    Hope you're having fun in the sun.

    Here's a drawing of the snow gnu I made. Just wanted you to see what you're missing, and to tell you how much I miss you—and your bedtime stories and gnu-house cookies.

Love ya, XXXXXXXXX,

Your grand-gnu-son,

Nicky

Another thoughtful time to write is when something especially sad—or wonderful—happens. Everyone relishes a friend who knows how you feel, and sympathizes—or celebrates—with you.

Dear Leo,

I was sorry to hear Pokey your pet turtle died. I know how much you loved him. You can come over and look at Goldy Fish anytime. He's not the same but it might help.

See ya,
Nicky

Hi, Gloria,

Congratulations on being the first girl giraffe in the Basketball Hall of Fame. You're really up there, and I'm proud of you.

Wow! and keep the ball rolling!

N

VISITING

Consideration and flexibility are key words when visiting.

WHEN YOU VISIT

When Nicky Gnu visits Max Monkey, he tries to fit into the family routine and the bed. It isn't like home, but that's part of the fun.

He picks up after himself. He offers to help peel bananas and walk Max's pet iguana.

He amuses himself, without snooping, when Max has to answer the phone.

He puts his soda glass on a coaster so the furniture isn't ruined, and he doesn't finger Max's fragile miniature spacemen collection.

He says, "I'd love to try it," when Max suggests something new to eat or do.

WHEN A FRIEND SLEEPS OVER

When Nicky has Max overnight he is a good host. He tries to make Max at home in his home.

He tries to think of things Max would like to play or eat. He makes sure there are plenty of bananas, and pulls out Jungle Jamboree, because that's Max's favorite game.

As soon as Max arrives, he shows him where the bathroom is and where to hang his pajamas.

He asks Max if he would like anything to be more comfortable. When Max says, "a night light," he understands. Because that's what friends are for. And visits are for making good friends even better.

EAT NICELY

BASIC GOOD TABLE MANNERS

Nicky knows that good table manners make meals more pleasant.

He washes his paws, combs his hair, and tidies up when Gram Gnu announces, "Lunch is almost ready."

When she calls, "Come," he does. Gram Gnu's stew is tastier hot and she is pleased with Nicky's promptness. Nicky lets Gram Gnu go into the dining room first and holds her chair.

At the table he sits up straight, unfolds his napkin on his lap, and listens attentively to what Gram Gnu has to say.

Hungry as he is, he waits for Gram Gnu to take the first bite—because it's polite. It's also a clue as to which spoon to use.

When he's finished dessert, Nicky puts his dessert fork neatly on the plate, and tells Gram Gnu everything was delicious.

He offers to help with the dishes and Gram Gnu gratefully accepts.

54

G N U R U L E

What you use first goes on the outside. The soup or stew spoon goes outside the teaspoon, and the dinner fork goes outside the dessert fork. Knives are placed closest to the plate, with the sharp side on the inside.

When he helps set the table Nicky says to himself, "The knives and spoons and glasses are always right," which is just where he puts them.

Which leaves the napkin, forks, and butter plates on the left.

TABLE TIPS

Nicky Gnu uses his napkin to wipe away his milk mustache after he drinks.

Wanda Warthog passes the milk pitcher around, not across the table. She holds it securely so Oopsa Elephant can take it by the handle and nothing will spill.

Leo Lion holds the serving spoon in his right paw and takes a small helping of Mrs. Gnu's swamp-grass soufflé. He knows that trying new dishes is part of the fun of eating, even though he prefers meat. After serving himself, he puts the serving spoon back securely in the dish.

Gogo Tiger asks for seconds of sticky buns after everyone has had firsts. He says, "Please pass," instead of reaching with his long paws. He takes the closest bun, not the biggest or stickiest.

Prissa Panther interrupts the table talk to point and yell, "Yoo-hoo, everybody, Annie Anteater has a clump of green swamp grass on her snout." Prissa should have been more thoughtful and whispered to Annie, "You may not know it, but . . ." Now Annie is embarrassed in front of everyone.

Iggy Ape is an eyesore and an accident about to happen. He chews with his mouth open, wipes his greasy paws on the tablecloth, and rudely yells, "The sauce looks like squished wiggle worms."

Then he reaches across the table to grab the syrup pitcher and spills it all over the tablecloth. Iggy will probably not be invited for lunch again.

PROBLEMS, PITFALLS, AND ACCIDENTS

Nicky Gnu is allergic to chocolate. It makes him all itchy and red. When offered chocolate cake, he says simply, "No thank you, I can't eat chocolate."

He leaves any that is already on his plate.

Gogo Tiger is left-pawed. He tries his best to keep his paws tucked in and apologizes if he accidentally bumps his neighbor.

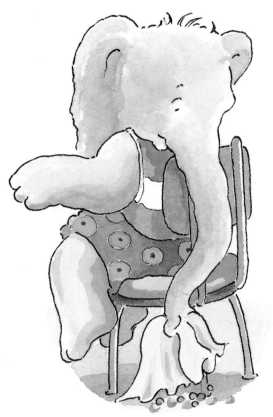

Uh-oh, Oopsa Elephant waves her trunk and knocks over the sweet peas.

She says, "I'm sorry," and shows it by helping to wipe up.

Gloria Giraffe gets a piece of swamp grass stuck in her braces. She quietly excuses herself and goes to the bathroom to remove it in private.

Iggy screams, "THERE'S A WIGGLE WORM IN MY AL- PHABET SOUP!" throws his soup cup, and gets soup all over.

The polite way would have been to point out the problem quietly to his host or hostess and ask for a fresh cup.

IN A RESTAURANT

Eating out is an adventure Nicky Gnu enjoys. He takes special care to look nice and practice his best table manners.

He discusses the menu with his parents. He tells them what he wants and they tell the waitress.

Nicky sits up straight, listens to what Sis Gnu is saying, and waits patiently for the food.

It will come, and so will his turn to talk.

I know what to do. We'll trade.

When what he ordered isn't what he expected, Nicky takes a couple of trying bites.

When he really can't eat it, he whispers to his parents, who see to it that he gets something he likes.

Unlike the ape at the next table, he doesn't do anything to annoy the other diners, who nod, "What a nice polite gnu. What an appalling ape!"

END NOTE

Iggy Ape has been having a bad time for a long time. Everyone has been avoiding him in the playground, and he's no longer invited to parties.

He takes a long look at his bad-mannered self in the mirror and has a rude shock. He realizes he is to blame for his own bad times.

He straightens up, washes up, and looks for Nicky Gnu.

"I'm sorry I've been such an ill-mannered ape face!" Iggy tells Nicky. "I want to apologize for being rude to you, Gnu. I'd like to change and for us to be friends—if it isn't too late."

"It's never too late, and I appreciate your apology," Nicky says with a smile and holds out his paw.

Iggy smiles back and shakes Nicky's paw. What a nice difference when he smiles!

"Good manners come naturally with practice. You, too, can be positively polite. You'll see," Nicky says as they go off together to a fun-filled future.